Best Ever Fruit Cobbler & Crisp Recipes

Lori Burke

Table of Contents

Legal Information

First Printing: 2012
ISBN-13: 978-1481845502
ISBN-10: 1481845500
Printed in the United States of America

Dedication

Dedicated to my Mother-in-law & Sister-in-law who are two of the best bakers I know

Hello!

My Mother-in-law and Sister-in-law introduced me to cobblers and crisps years ago. These are wonderful deep dish fruit desserts with golden brown top crusts. They're made from scratch with fresh fruit and natural ingredients.

Fruit cobblers and crisps are surprisingly quick and easy to make. They are wonderful desserts to serve during the cold winter months. Served warm with ice cream or flavored whipped cream, they are sure to chase away the winter blahs.

Homemade cobblers and crisps go back to Colonial America and were originally served for breakfast or as a main course. It wasn't until the late 1800s that cobblers, crisps and related pastry and fruit dishes were treated as desserts.

A cobbler has a deep-dish fruit filling and a thick top crust. The top crust can be either biscuit-like or cake-like. The biscuit dough or cobbler batter is usually dropped in spoonsful on top of the fruit. It's said the name "cobbler" comes from the fact that the baked biscuit topping looks like cobblestones.

Traditional fruit cobblers use biscuit dough for the topping. Another variation of cobbler uses a batter made with self-rising flour (or flour and baking powder), salt, sugar, milk and eggs. The batter is poured over hot butter and topped with a fruit filling. It rises to form a more cake-like crust that covers the fruit filling. My family prefers this type of cobbler because the cake-like crust is moister than biscuit crusts.

A crisp has a fruit filling on the bottom with a crispy top crust usually made of oats, sugar, butter and sometimes nuts. The crisp topping is crunchier than a cobbler crust.

Both cobblers and crisps are wonderful served warm with ice cream or whipped cream toppings. In **Best Ever Fruit Cobbler & Crisp Recipes** I've included 15 fruit cobbler recipes, 15 fruit crisp recipes and 5 whipped cream toppings. They are all bake from scratch recipes and extremely fast and easy to make. I really hope you'll enjoy this new collection of cobbler and crisp recipes!

Lori Burke

About the Author

Lori Burke is a wife and mother who lives with her family near Chicago Illinois. As a child she first learned how to bake from her Polish and Italian grandmothers. After she married and had two children, Lori searched for great desserts to serve to her family. Because of a full-time job and busy schedule, she didn't have time to bake time-consuming desserts.

So Lori started to develop and collect dessert recipes that met 3 criteria: easy to make, quick to prepare and consistently delicious.

At the urging of her husband and two kids Lori published her first dessert cookbook, 30 Delicious Refrigerator Cake Recipes, in January 2012. It quickly became an Amazon best seller. She has enjoyed the same success with her seven other dessert cookbooks.

Lori believes that a great dessert improves anyone's day!

Other Lori Burke Cookbooks

Best Ever Christmas Dessert Recipes

41 traditional and contemporary Christmas dessert recipes that are perfect for your Christmas holidays

30 Delicious Poke Cake Recipes

Delicious cake, pudding, fresh fruit and whipped cream desserts

30 Delicious Dump Cake Recipes

Amazing, simple-to-make cobbler dessert

30 Delicious Icebox Cookie Recipes

Mouth-watering slice and bake icebox cookie recipes

30 Delicious Refrigerator Cake Recipes

Easy-to-make refrigerator cake recipes, the majority of which require no baking

30 Delicious Family Favorite Recipes

Cake recipes Lori bakes for her family and friends

30 Delicious Ice Cream Cake Recipes

Delicious ice cream cakes you can make at home

30 Delicious Brownie & Bar Recipes

Brownie and bar recipes that the entire family will enjoy

Facebook Fan Page

I have a Facebook Fan Page called Lori Burke's Kitchen.   I share recipes there and we chat about baking.   Here's a link to Lori Burke's Kitchen:

http://www.facebook.com/LoriJBurke

COBBLER RECIPES

Apple Cobbler

Wonderful apple cobbler that uses a traditional technique but creates a cobbler with a more contemporary cake-like topping.

Servings: 6 to 8

Ingredients

1/2 cup of granulated sugar
1/4 cup dark brown sugar
2 teaspoons of ground cinnamon
1 teaspoon vanilla extract
1 cup of chopped pecans, divided
5 cups of Granny Smith apples
1 tablespoon of fresh lemon juice
1/3 cup of unsalted butter, melted
1 cup of self rising flour
1 cup of granulated sugar
1 egg
1/2 cup of milk

Directions

Preheat oven to 325 ° F. Butter an 8-inch x 8-inch glass baking dish.

Filling

In a medium bowl mix together the 1/2 cup of the granulated sugar, the brown sugar, cinnamon, vanilla extract and half of the pecans.

Peel, core and slice the apples. Put them in a large bowl. Sprinkle with the lemon juice and toss the apples.   Turn the apples into the prepared baking dish.   Pour the Cinnamon-Sugar   mixture   over   the   apples.

Topping

Melt the butter and set aside.

Sift the flour into a small bowl. Take 1 cup of the sifted flour and resift with the 1 cup of granulated sugar into a large bowl. Add the egg, milk and melted butter to the flour-sugar mixture. Mix until combined.

Drop the batter by spoonsful over the apples. Sprinkle the remaining   pecans   over   the   batter.

Bake at 325° F. for 50 minutes to one hour or until light brown. Rotate the dish 180° halfway through baking.

Remove from the oven and cool for 10 to 15 minutes.

Serve warm with ice cream or Sweetened Whipped Cream (See the Sweetened Whipped Cream recipe in the Whipped Toppings Section).

Apricot Cobbler

This cobbler has more of a cake-like topping.

Servings: 6 to 8

Ingredients

Filling
1 lb. fresh apricots, pitted, peeled and cut in half
1/8 teaspoon nutmeg
3 tablespoons Amaretto, divided (or another almond liqueur)
1 tablespoon sugar

Topping
1 cup flour
1 cup sugar
1/2 teaspoon salt
2 teaspoons baking powder
1/4 cup chilled unsalted butter
1 egg
1/2 cup milk

Directions

Preheat the oven to 350° F. Butter a 9-inch baking dish.

Filling

Prepare the apricots and place them in a large bowl.

Sprinkle the apricots with nutmeg, 2 tablespoons Amaretto and 1 tablespoon of sugar and toss lightly. Set the bowl aside.

Topping

Sift the flour into a separate, large bowl. Add the 1 cup of sugar, salt and baking powder to the flour. Whisk the dry ingredients until mixed.

Use a pastry blender to cut the butter into the flour mixture until crumbly.

In a small bowl mix together the egg, milk and remaining 1 tablespoon Amaretto.

Add the egg mixture into the flour mixture. Mix with a fork.

Drop the batter by spoonsful over the top of the apricots.

Bake for 35 to 45 minutes or until the crust has browned. Rotate the dish 180° halfway through baking.

Remove the cobbler from the oven and cool for 5 to 10 minutes.

Serve warm with Sweetened Whipped Cream or ice cream. (See the Sweetened Whipped Cream recipe in the Whipped Toppings Section).

Berry Berry Cobbler

In this delicious cobbler recipe the berries are spooned on top of the cobbler batter. After baking you have a wonderful golden crust and sweet berries.

Servings: 6 to 8

Ingredients

Filling

3 cups of combined fresh mixed berries (blackberries, raspberries, blueberries), rinsed
3/4 cup sugar

Topping

1 cup flour
3/4 cup sugar
2 teaspoons baking powder
1/2 teaspoon salt
1 cup milk
1 stick of unsweetened butter, melted

Directions

Preheat oven to 375° F.
Butter an 8-inch x 8-inch baking dish.

Filling

Pour the mixed berries into a large bowl. Add the 3/4 cup sugar. Stir until the sugar is combined. Set the berries aside.

Topping

Sift the flour into a large bowl. Add the sugar, baking powder and salt. Whisk to combine.

Pour in the milk. Stir until the ingredients are all combined. Pour the melted butter into the batter. Stir until the butter is combined. Pour the batter into the prepared baking dish.

Assemble the Cobbler

Drop spoonsful of the berry mixture on top of the batter. Don't stir.

Bake for 35 minutes or until golden brown. Rotate the dish 180° halfway through baking.

Remove from the oven and cool for 5 to 10 minutes.

Serve plain or with ice cream or with Sweetened Whipped Cream. (See the Sweetened Whipped Cream recipe in the Whipped Toppings Section).

Notes

You can also make this cobbler with frozen berries. Just measure the berries after they're defrosted.

Black Raspberry Cobbler

This is my Mother-in-Law's traditional Black Raspberry cobbler recipe with a rolled dough top crust

Servings: 6 to 8

Ingredients

1 quart black raspberries
1/2 cup sugar
2 tablespoons flour
1 tablespoon lemon juice
1 cup all-purpose flour
1/2 teaspoon salt
1-1/4 teaspoons baking powder
1/4 cup unsalted butter
1/2 cup milk minus 1 tablespoon

Directions

Filling

Preheat oven to 450° F. Butter a deep dish pie pan.

Wash and drain the raspberries. Put them into a large bowl.

Combine the sugar and 2 tablespoons of flour. Pour this mixture over the raspberries and stir. Add the lemon juice. Stir again. Pour the berry mixture into the prepared pie pan.

Topping

In a separate bowl sift the flour. Re-measure 1 cup of the sifted flour. Resift the flour, salt and baking powder. Cut the butter in with a pastry cutter or 2 knives.

Add the milk all at once. Stir with a fork until the dough holds together.

Turn the dough out onto a floured working space. Roll the dough to a 1/4-inch thickness.

Place the rolled out dough on top of the berries. Trim the edged of the dough to fit.   Cut a design in the center of the dough to allow steam to escape.

Bake in the 450° F. oven for 15 minutes. Reduce heat to 325° F. Rotate the pan 180°.

Continue baking for 20 minutes until the berries are cooked through.

Remove from the oven and cool for 10 minutes on a rack. Serve warm with ice cream or with Sweetened Whipped Cream. (See the Sweetened Whipped Cream recipe in the Whipped Toppings Section).

Blueberry Cobbler

Servings: 6 to 8

Ingredients

Filling
6 cups fresh blueberries
3 tablespoons fresh squeezed orange juice
1/3 cup sugar
3 tablespoons cornstarch

Topping
3/4 cup unbleached flour
1/3 cup oat bran
1/3 cup sugar
1-1/2 teaspoons baking powder
3/4 cup buttermilk

Directions

Preheat the oven to 375° F.

Butter a 2-1/2 quart casserole dish.

Dump the blueberries into a large bowl. Sprinkle the orange juice over the berries and toss.

Add the sugar and cornstarch to the berry mixture. Stir gently to mix. Set aside for 1/2 hour. After 1/2 hour stir gently again to mix the berries and juices. Pour the berries into the prepared casserole dish.

Sift the flour into a large bowl. Add the oat bran, sugar and baking powder. Stir together until all the dry ingredients are mixed well.

Add the buttermilk and stir until the ingredients are combined.

Use a tablespoon to drop the batter on top of the blueberry mixture.

Bake for 45 minutes or until the crust has browned. Rotate the baking dish 180° halfway through baking.

Remove the cobbler from the oven. Let it cool for 5 to 10 minutes.

Serve plain or with ice cream or Sweetened Whipped Cream. (See the Sweetened Whipped Cream recipe in the Whipped Toppings Section).

Blueberry-Peach Cobbler

Servings: 6 to 8

Ingredients

5 cups sliced peeled peaches
3 tablespoons quick-cooking tapioca
1/2 cup granulated sugar
1 cups blueberries
1 tablespoon baking powder
2-1/2 cups flour
6 tablespoons unsalted butter
1 to 1-1/2 cups buttermilk

Directions

Preheat the oven to 400° F. Butter a 2-1/2 quart glass baking dish.

<u>Filling</u>
Add the peaches, tapioca and sugar to the baking dish. Stir well.

Bake the peaches in the preheated oven for 10 minutes. Add the blueberries to the peaches. Mix with a spoon. Heat for 5 more minutes. Remove from the oven.

<u>Topping</u>

Sift the baking powder and flour into a large bowl.
Cut in the butter with a pastry cutter. The mixture should be like coarse meal.

Add 1 cup of the buttermilk and stir with fork. Add more milk a little at a time until you have a smoother batter.

Drop tablespoonfuls of the batter on top of the fruit. Return to the oven for 20 to 25 minutes or until the batter has browned.

Remove from the oven and cool for 5 to 10 minutes.

Serve plain or with Sweetened Whipped Cream or ice cream. (See the Sweetened Whipped Cream recipe in the Whipped Toppings Section).

Caramel Apple Raisin Cobbler

This is a wonderful cobbler that combines a spiced apple and raisin filling, a cake-like crust and caramel topping for garnish.

Servings: 6 to 8

Ingredients

<u>Topping</u>
1 cup of self rising flour
1 cup of granulated sugar
1 egg
1/2 cup of milk
1/3 cup of unsalted butter, melted

<u>Filling</u>
1/2 cup packed brown sugar
2 tablespoons cornstarch
1/4 teaspoon ground ginger
1 teaspoon cinnamon
1/8 teaspoon nutmeg
1 1/4 cups water
1/4 cup raisins
6 cups sliced peeled Granny Smith apples
1 tablespoon lemon juice, fresh squeezed
1 teaspoon lemon zest
1 tablespoon unsalted butter
1 tablespoon granulated sugar

<u>Garnish</u>
Caramel topping

Directions

<u>Topping</u>
Sift the flour into a medium bowl.

Take 1 cup of the sifted flour and resift with the 1 cup granulated sugar into a large bowl.

Add the egg, milk and melted butter to the flour-sugar mixture.
 Mix until combined.

<u>Filling</u>

Preheat the oven to 425° F.

Butter a 2-quart casserole dish.

In a large saucepan add the brown sugar, cornstarch, ginger, cinnamon and nutmeg. Stir until combined.

Stir in the water and raisins.   Cook and stir until the mixture thickens and bubbles.

Add in the apples, lemon juice, lemon zest and butter. Stir well.

Cook for 5 minutes.

Turn the apples into a 2-quart casserole dish.

Assemble the Cobbler

Stir the topping you prepared earlier. Drop heaping spoonsful of the topping over the hot apples until all of the topping has been used.

Sprinkle the topping with granulated sugar.

Bake in the preheated oven for 20 to 25 minutes or until the crust is browned. Rotate the dish 180° halfway through cooking.

Cool for 5 to 10 minutes.

Serve warm with vanilla bean ice cream and caramel topping.

Cranberry Apple Cobbler

Apples and cranberries make a great combination in a cobbler.

Servings: 6 to 8

Ingredients

<u>Filling</u>

3/4 cup granulated sugar
3/4 cup brown sugar
1 cup fresh cranberries
3 tablespoons quick-cooking tapioca
1/2 teaspoon ground cinnamon
1/8 teaspoon nutmeg
1 cup water
5 cups Cortland or Granny Smith apples, cored, peeled and sliced
2 tablespoons unsalted butter

<u>Topping</u>

3/4 cup all-purpose flour
2 tablespoons granulated sugar
1 teaspoon baking powder
1/8 teaspoon salt
1/4 cup cold unsalted butter, cubed
1/4 cup milk

Directions

Preheat oven to 350° F. Butter a 2-1/2 quart glass baking dish

In a large saucepan mix the white sugar, brown sugar, cranberries, tapioca, cinnamon, nutmeg and water. Stir until all of the ingredients are combined.

Add the apples and stir to coat.

Cook over medium heat and keep stirring until the mixture boils. Cook and stir for 4 more minutes.

Pour the apple mixture into the baking dish. Slice the butter into thin pats and put on top of the apples.

Put the flour, sugar, baking powder and salt into a large bowl. Cut in the butter with a pastry blender or 2 knives until crumbly.

Stir in the milk until the dough forms. Drop tablespoons of the dough over apple mixture.

Bake uncovered at 350° F. for 1 hour or until topping is golden brown. Rotate the dish 180° halfway through cooking.

Take out of the oven and cool on a rack for 5 to 10 minutes.

Serve warm with Sweetened Whipped Cream or ice cream. (See the Sweetened Whipped Cream recipe in the Whipped Toppings Section).

Notes

You can also use frozen cranberries. Just measure the cranberries after they've defrosted.

Mango Cobbler

Servings: 8 to 10

Ingredients

<u>Filling</u>
2/3 cup sugar
1 tablespoon cornstarch
1 cup water
3 cups sliced firm, ripe mangoes
1/2 teaspoon ground nutmeg
1/2 teaspoon finely chopped crystallized ginger
1 teaspoon lemon juice
1-1/2 teaspoons unsalted butter
1 tablespoon granulated sugar mixed with 1 teaspoon cinnamon

<u>Topping</u>
1 cup flour
1/3 cup brown sugar
1 1/2 teaspoon baking powder
1/2 teaspoon salt
3 tablespoons unsalted butter
1/2 cup milk

Directions

Preheat the oven to 375° F.

Add the 2/3 cup sugar and cornstarch together in a medium saucepan and whisk to combine.

Gradually stir in the water, mangoes, and nutmeg, crystallized ginger and lemon juice. Heat for 20 minutes on low, stirring periodically.

Pour the mango mixture into 9-inch x 9-inch baking dish. Top with pats of butter and sprinkle sugar cinnamon mixture over the top.

Stir together the flour, brown sugar, baking powder and salt. Cut in the butter until the mixture resembles coarse meal.

Stir in the milk and mix the batter thoroughly.

Drop spoonfuls of batter on top of the hot fruit.

Bake in the preheated oven for 35 minutes to 40 minutes. Rotate the dish 180° halfway through cooking.

Serve warm with ice cream or Rum Whipped Cream. (See the Rum Whipped Cream recipe in the Whipped Toppings Section).

Old Fashioned Cherry Cobbler

This is another of my Mother-in-Law's cobbler recipes. It's more of a pie technique that uses biscuit dough.

Servings: 6 to 8

Ingredients

Filling
3 cups pitted sour red cherries
1 cup canned sour red cherry juice
3 tablespoons quick-cooking tapioca
3/4 cups granulated sugar
2 tablespoons melted unsalted butter

Biscuit Dough
2 cups sifted all-purpose flour
2 teaspoons baking powder
1/2 teaspoon salt
4 tablespoons unsalted butter, chilled
3/4 cup cold milk

Directions

Butter a 10-inch deep dish pie pan.
Preheat oven to 450° F.

Filling

In a medium bowl combine the cherries and cherry juice.

In a separate bowl combine the tapioca, sugar and melted butter. Add the tapioca mixture to the cherry mixture and stir until combined. Turn the cherry mixture into the pie pan.

Biscuit dough

Sift the flour, baking powder and salt together. Cut in the butter with 2 knives or a pastry cutter until the consistency is like coarse meal.

Stir in the cold milk until the dough holds together. Transfer the dough to a lightly floured board and knead for 30 seconds.

Roll the biscuit dough 1/4-inch thick. Cut a round section that is large enough to cover the pie dish. Place the round over the top of the apples. Press the dough against the edges of the baking dish to seal. Cut slits in the top.

Bake for 10 minutes at 450° F. Reduce the heat to 350° F. And bake for 10 to 15 minutes longer.

Serve warm or cold. Top with powdered sugar, Sweetened Whipped Cream or ice cream. (See the Sweetened Whipped Cream recipe in the Whipped Toppings Section).

Notes

If you have any biscuit dough left roll the dough out to 1/2-inch thickness. Cut into 2-inch rounds with a biscuit cutter or glass. Bake on an ungreased cookie sheet in a 450° F. oven for 12 to 15 minutes.

Peach Cobbler

In this Peach Cobbler the batter is poured into hot butter and then the fruit is spooned on top of the batter.

Servings: 6 to 8

Ingredients

Filling
2 cups fresh peaches, peeled and sliced
3/4 cup sugar

Crust
1/2 stick unsalted butter
3/4 cup flour
3/4 cup sugar
2 teaspoons baking powder
1/8 teaspoon salt
1/2 teaspoon ground cinnamon
1/8 teaspoon nutmeg
3/4 cup buttermilk

Directions

Preheat the oven to 350 degrees F.

Put the peaches into a large bowl. Sprinkle the sugar over the peaches. Toss the peaches to spread the sugar. Set the bowl aside.

Sift the flour into a large bowl. Add the sugar, baking powder, salt, cinnamon and nutmeg. Whisk to combine. Add the buttermilk and stir until the batter is combined. Set aside.

Slice the butter into pats and put the pats in an 8-inch baking dish. Put the dish into the oven to melt the butter.

After the butter has melted take the dish out of the oven. Make sure the butter is evenly spread on the bottom of the dish.

Stir the batter and pour it over the hot butter. Do not stir.

Spoon the peach slices and juices over the batter.

Bake for 45 to 55 minutes or until golden on top. Rotate the dish 180° halfway through cooking.

Remove the pan from the oven. Cool on a rack for 5 to 10 minutes.

Serve warm. You can serve plain or with Brandy Whipped Cream or ice cream. (See the Brandy Whipped Cream recipe in the Whipped Toppings Section).

Peach Cobbler II

In this peach cobbler recipe the peaches are cooked with sugar and spices before baking.

Servings: 10 to 12+

Ingredients

Filling
5 cups fresh peaches, sliced
2 teaspoons lemon juice
1/3 cup granulated sugar
3/4 teaspoon ground cinnamon
1/8 teaspoon ground nutmeg

Crust
1 cup all-purpose flour
1 cup granulated sugar
1/4 teaspoon salt
2 teaspoons baking powder
1 egg
3/4 cup milk
1 teaspoon vanilla extract
1/2 cup unsalted butter

Directions

Preheat   the   oven   to   350°   F.

<u>Filling</u>

Put the peaches and lemon juice in a large saucepan. Stir the peaches.

Add the sugar, cinnamon and nutmeg to the peaches and bring to a boil. Stir periodically. Take the pan off of the heat and   set   aside.

<u>Crust</u>

Sift the flour into a large bowl. Add the sugar, salt and baking powder. Stir to combine.   Add the egg, milk and vanilla extract. Mix until you have a smooth batter.

Cut the butter into pats. Spread the butter pats in the bottom of a 9-inch x 13-inch baking dish. Put the dish in the oven to melt the butter.

Take the dish out of the oven once the butter has melted.

Pour the batter over the butter in the baking dish. Don't stir.

Spoon the peach mixture evenly on top of the batter but don't   stir.

Bake for 45 to 55 minutes or until golden brown. Rotate the dish 180° halfway through cooking.

Remove from the oven and cool on a rack for 5 to 10 minutes.

Serve warm. You can serve the cobbler plain, with ice cream or with Sweetened Whipped Cream. (See the Sweetened Whipped Cream recipe in the Whipped Toppings Section).

Pear Brandy Cobbler

In this peach cobbler recipe the peaches are cooked with sugar and spices before baking and the crust is cake-like.

Servings: 6 to 8

Ingredients

Filling
5 fresh, ripe pears (Bartlett or Anjou), peeled, cored and cut into 1-inch pieces
1 cup sugar

Crust

1 cup flour
1 cup sugar
2 teaspoons baking powder
1 teaspoon cinnamon
1/4 teaspoon salt
1/2 cup milk
1/4 cup brandy
1 egg
1/2 cup unsalted butter

Directions

Preheat the oven to 325° F.

<u>Filling</u>

Put the pears in a large bowl. Sprinkle them with 1 cup of sugar, toss and set aside.

<u>Crust</u>

Sift the flour into a separate, large bowl. Add the 1 cup of sugar, baking powder, cinnamon and salt. Whisk to blend well.

In a medium bowl, add the milk, brandy and egg. Stir well.

Slowly pour the milk mixture into the dry mixture and stir until a batter forms.

Put the butter into a 2-quart casserole. Place the casserole dish into the preheated oven until the butter melts. Remove from the oven but keep the oven set at 325° F.

Pour the batter over the melted butter in the casserole dish. Do not stir.

Spoon the pears over the batter. Do not stir.

Bake in the preheated oven for 50 to 60 minutes or until the crust is golden brown. Rotate the casserole dish 180° halfway through cooking.

Remove from the oven and cool for 5 to 10 minutes.

Serve warm. Serve plain or with Brandy Whipped cream or ice cream. (See the Brandy Whipped Cream recipe in the Whipped Toppings Section).

Raspberry Cobbler

This is my sister-in-law's Raspberry Cobbler recipe. She got it from a magazine over 15 years ago and has tweaked it. It's simple and delicious.

Servings: 6 to 8

Ingredients

1 cup self-rising flour
1 cup sugar
1 cup cold milk
3/4 teaspoon almond extract
5 cups of raspberries
1/2 cup unsalted butter

Directions

Preheat oven to 375° F.

In a large bowl combine the flour and sugar. Whisk to combine. Add the milk and almond extract to the flour mixture. Blend until the batter is smooth.

Melt the butter in a 12-inch x 8-inch baking pan.

Spoon the batter over the hot butter.

Spoon the raspberries on top of the batter.

Bake in the preheated oven for 35 minutes or until the crust has risen and is golden brown. Rotate the pan 180° halfway through cooking.

Remove from the oven and cool for 5 to 10 minutes.

Serve warm. You can enjoy it plain or with ice cream or Sweetened Whipped Cream. (See the Sweetened Whipped Cream recipe in the Whipped Toppings Section).

Strawberry Cobbler

Servings: 8 to 10

Ingredients

Filling
6 cups strawberries, hulled and sliced
1 cup sugar

Topping
2 cups flour
3/4 cup sugar
1 tablespoons baking powder
1/2 teaspoon real salt
1-1/4 cups milk
2 teaspoons vanilla extract
1/2 cup unsalted butter

Directions

Preheat the oven to 325° F.

Add the strawberries to a large bowl. Sprinkle 1 cup of sugar over the strawberries and toss. Set aside.

Sift the flour into a large bowl. Add the remaining 3/4 cup sugar, baking powder and salt to the flour. Whisk to mix.

Add the milk and vanilla to the flour mixture and stir until the dough is smooth.

Place the 1/2 cup butter in a 9-inch x 9-inch square baking dish and melt in the preheated oven. When the butter has melted remove the dish from the oven.

Pour the batter over the melted butter. Do not stir.

Spoon the strawberries over the top of batter. Do not stir.

Bake for 55 minutes to 1 hour until the cobbler crust is golden brown. Rotate the dish 180° halfway through cooking.

Remove from the oven and cool for 5 to 10 minutes.

Serve warm. Serve plain or with Sweetened Whipped Cream or ice cream. (See the Sweetened Whipped Cream recipe in the Whipped Toppings Section).

CRISPS

Apple Crisp

Servings: 10 to 12+

Ingredients

Filling

3 large Golden Delicious apples & 3 Rome apples
Fresh-squeezed lemon juice (1 lemon)
3/4 cup all-purpose flour
1/4 cup sugar
3/4 teaspoon ground cinnamon

Crisp

1 cup all-purpose flour
1-1/4 cups rolled oats
1/2 cup packed dark brown sugar
1 teaspoon ground cinnamon
1 cup pecans, coarsely chopped
8 tablespoons cold unsalted butter, cut into small pieces

Directions

Preheat the oven to 350 ° F. Move the oven rack to the center of the oven.

Filling

Butter a 9-inch x 13-inch baking dish.

Peel, core, and dice the apples into medium cubes. Add the apples to a large mixing bowl. Sprinkle the apples with the lemon juice and toss to coat.

In a medium bowl sift together the flour and sugar. Whisk to mix.

Add the flour-sugar mixture to the apples. Stir the apples well until the flour mixture is absorbed. Turn the apples into the prepared baking dish. Use a spatula to even out the apples.

Crisp

In another large bowl, mix together the flour, oats, sugar, cinnamon, and nuts.

Cut the butter into the flour mixture with a pastry cutter. The mixture should be coarse.

Sprinkle the flour mixture over the apples.

Bake for 45 minutes until the topping is light brown. Rotate the dish 180° halfway through cooking.

Remove from the oven and cool for 10 minutes.

Serve warm with vanilla ice cream or Sweetened Whipped Cream. (See the Sweetened Whipped Cream recipe in the Whipped Toppings Section).

Apple Cranberry Pear Crisp

Servings: 10 To 12

Ingredients

<u>Filling</u>

5 cups Granny Smith apples, peeled, cored and thinly sliced
4 cups pears, peeled, cored and thinly sliced
2 tablespoons freshly squeezed lemon juice
1-1/2 cups cranberries
1/4 cup light brown sugar
3/4 cups granulated white sugar, divided
1 tablespoon all-purpose flour
1 teaspoon ground cinnamon

<u>Crisp</u>

1/2 cup granulated sugar
1 cup light brown sugar, lightly packed
1/2 teaspoon ground cinnamon
1 cup all-purpose flour
1/2 cup unsalted butter, chilled
1-1/4 cups old fashioned oats
1 teaspoon pure vanilla extract

Directions

Preheat oven to 350 ° F. Butter a 9-inch x 13-inch baking dish.

<u>Filling</u>

Put the sliced apples and pears into a large bowl. Add the lemon juice and toss to coat. Add the cranberries. Stir to mix.

In a separate bowl add the brown sugar, white sugar, flour and cinnamon. Whisk to mix. Pour the sugar mixture over the fruit. Stir well.

Pour the fruit into the prepared baking dish. Use a spatula to even out the fruit.

<u>Crisp</u>

Add the granulated sugar, brown sugar and cinnamon into a medium bowl. Whisk to mix. Sprinkle over the fruit mixture.

Sift the flour into a medium bowl. Stir in the vanilla extract. Cut the butter into the flour. The mixture should be coarse.

Stir in the oats.

Spread the topping over the apple, pear, cranberry mixture.

Bake in preheated oven for 45-50 minutes or until topping is light brown. Rotate the dish 180° halfway through cooking.

Remove from the oven and cool for 10 to 15 minutes.

Serve warm with vanilla ice cream or Sweetened Whipped Cream. (See the Sweetened Whipped Cream recipe in the Whipped Toppings Section).

Apple Pecan Crisp

Servings: 6 to 8

Ingredients

Filling
7 cups Granny Smith apples, peeled & sliced
1 tablespoon lemon juice, fresh squeezed
1/2 cup granulated sugar
2 teaspoons cinnamon
1/2 cup packed dark brown sugar

Crisp
3/4 cup flour
1/2 teaspoon pure vanilla extract
1 cup chopped pecans
1/2 cup unsalted butter, softened

Directions

Preheat the oven to 350° F.

Butter an 8-inch x 8-inch baking dish.

Filling

Put the apples in a large bowl. Sprinkle with the lemon juice and toss the apples. Transfer the apples to the buttered baking dish.

Mix the granulated sugar, cinnamon and brown sugar together in a small bowl. Sprinkle the cinnamon-sugar mixture over apples.

Crisp

Sift the flour into a large bowl. Add the vanilla extract.

Add the chopped nuts to the flour and stir to mix.

Cut the butter into the flour using a pastry cutter or two knives. The texture should be coarse and crumbly.

Sprinkle the flour mixture over the apples.

Bake the apple crisp in the oven for 35 to 45 minutes, or until the apples are tender and the topping is a golden brown. Rotate the dish 180° halfway through cooking.

Remove the crisp from the oven and cool for 5 to 10 minutes.

Serve warm with ice cream or Sweetened Whipped Cream. (See the Sweetened Whipped Cream recipe in the Whipped Toppings Section).

Apple Raspberry Crisp

Servings: 6 to 8

Ingredients

<u>Filling</u>
3 cups baking apples, (Cortland, Granny Smith or Empire apples are all good)
2 cups raspberries
4 tablespoons granulated sugar
2 tablespoons flour
1 teaspoon vanilla
1/4 teaspoon cinnamon
1/8 teaspoon nutmeg
Pinch of salt
2 tablespoons cold butter, cut into thin pats

<u>Crisp</u>
1/2 cup rolled oats
3/4 cup flour
1/2 cup light brown sugar
3/4 cup almonds, chopped
7 tablespoons unsalted butter, softened

Directions

Preheat the oven to 375°F. Butter a 2-quart shallow baking dish.

<u>Filling</u>

Core and peel the apples. Cut them into 1/2-inch to 3/4-inch chunks.

Add 2 cups of raspberries and gently mix with the apples.

In a medium bowl add the granulated sugar, flour, vanilla, nutmeg, cinnamon and salt. Whisk to combine the ingredients.

Sprinkle the sugar-flour mixture over the fruit. Stir and toss the apples and raspberries so that they are coated with the sugar-flour mixture.

Turn the fruit mixture into the baking dish. Top the fruit with pats of cold butter. Set aside.

<u>Crisp</u>

In a large bowl whisk together the rolled oats, flour, brown sugar and chopped almonds.

Cut the butter into the oats and flour mixture. Use a pastry cutter or your fingers. All of the dry ingredients should be moistened by the butter.

<u>Assemble the Dessert</u>

Sprinkle the topping evenly over the top of the fruit.

Bake 40 to 45 minutes or until the crumble has browned. Rotate the dish 180° halfway through cooking.

Remove from the oven and cool for 10 to 15 minutes.

Serve warm with ice cream or Sweetened Whipped Cream. (See the Sweetened Whipped Cream recipe in the Whipped Toppings Section).

Blueberry Crisp

Servings: 6 to 8

Ingredients

Blueberry Filling

2 pints fresh blueberries
1/2 cup granulated sugar
1 tablespoon cornstarch
2 tablespoons orange juice
1/2 teaspoon vanilla extract

Crisp

1 cup all-purpose flour
1/2 cup quick-cooking oats
1/2 cup light or dark brown sugar
1/3 cup chopped pecans
1/4 teaspoon cinnamon
1/2 teaspoon vanilla extract
1 stick unsalted butter, cut into cubes and softened

Directions

Preheat the oven to 375°F.   Butter an 8-inch x 8-inch baking dish.

Blueberry Filling

In a large bowl add the blueberries and granulated sugar. Toss gently (try to not break the berries.)   Add the cornstarch, orange juice and vanilla extract. Use a spatula to gently mix the berry mixture.   Pour the berries into the prepared baking dish.

Crisp

In a large bowl combine the flour, oats, brown sugar, pecans, cinnamon and vanilla extract. Stir to combine.

Use a pastry cutter to cut the butter into the flour mixture. The consistency should be like coarse meal.

Sprinkle the crumble over the top of the blueberries.

Bake for 25 to 35 minutes or until the berries are bubbling and the crumble has browned. Rotate the dish 180° halfway through cooking.

Take the dish out of the oven. Cool for 10 minutes.

Serve warm with vanilla bean ice cream or Lemon Whipped Cream.   (See the Lemon Whipped Cream recipe in the Whipped Toppings Section).

Blueberry Apple Crisp

Serves: 6 to 8

Ingredients

Filling
2 cups fresh blueberries, washed and drained
3 Granny Smith apples, diced into 1/2-inch cubes
2 teaspoon lemon juice
3 tablespoons granulated white sugar

Crisp
1/3 cup flour
1/3 cup packed brown sugar
1/2 teaspoon cinnamon
1/2 teaspoon baking powder
3/4 cup quick cooking rolled oats
1/2 cup almonds, sliced
Pinch of salt
1/2 stick softened unsalted butter

Directions

Preheat the oven to 375° F.

Butter an 8-inch x 8-inch square baking dish.

Filling

Add the blueberries and apples together in a large bowl. Stir. Sprinkle the lemon juice over the fruit and toss to coat. Pour the blueberries and apples into the baking dish. Sprinkle the fruit with the granulated sugar and set aside.

Crisp

Sift the flour into a large bowl.

Add the brown sugar, cinnamon, baking powder, oats, almonds and salt to the flour.   Whisk to combine.

Cut the butter into the flour mixture with a pastry blender or two knives. Stir with a fork until the mixture is crumbly.

Spread the flour mixture over the berries.

Bake for 40 to 45 minutes or until the crisp has browned. Rotate the dish 180° halfway through cooking.

Remove from the oven and cool for 5 to 10 minutes.

Serve warm with Lemon Whipped Cream or ice cream. (See the Lemon Whipped Cream recipe in the Whipped Toppings Section).

Blueberry Peach Crisp

Servings: 6 to 8

Ingredients

<u>Filling</u>
7 cups peaches, peeled and cut into chunks
2 cups blueberries
1 tablespoon lemon juice
3/4 cup granulated sugar
4 teaspoons cornstarch
Zest from 1 lemon
1/2 teaspoon salt
1/4 teaspoon vanilla extract
1/4 teaspoon cinnamon

<u>Crisp</u>
1/2 cup all purpose flour
1/2 cup oats
1/4 cup granulated sugar
1/3 cup brown sugar
1 teaspoon ground cinnamon
1/2 teaspoon salt
6 tablespoons cold butter, thin pats

Directions

<u>Filling</u>

Preheat oven to 375° F. Butter an 8-inch x 8-inch square baking dish.

Put the peaches and blueberries in a large bowl. Sprinkle the fruit with the lemon juice and toss to mix.

Add the granulated sugar to the fruit and toss to mix.

In a medium bowl add the cornstarch, lemon zest, salt, vanilla extract and cinnamon. Whisk to mix.

Pour the sugar mixture over the fruit. Stir the fruit so that the cornstarch and other ingredients are combined.

Transfer to the baking dish. Set aside.

Crisp

Put the flour, oats, granulated sugar, brown sugar, cinnamon and salt into a large bowl. Whisk to mix well.

Cut the cold butter into the flour mixture with a pastry cutter or your fingers. The mixture should be coarse.

Spread the topping on top of the fruit in the baking dish.

Bake in the preheated oven for 40 to 50 minutes or until the fruit bubbles and the topping has browned. Rotate the dish 180° halfway through cooking.

Remove from the oven and cool for 10 to 15 minutes.

Serve warm with ice cream or Lemon Whipped Cream. (See the Lemon Whipped Cream recipe in the Whipped Toppings Section).

Cherry Crisp

Servings: 6 to 8

Ingredients

Filling
4 cups fresh pitted cherries
3/4 cup water
3/4 cup sugar
2-1/2 tablespoons cornstarch

Crisp
1/2 cup white sugar
1/4 cup brown sugar
1/3 cup flour
1/3 cup rolled oats
1/4 teaspoon cinnamon
1/8 teaspoon salt
6 tablespoons unsalted butter, melted

Directions

Heat the oven to 375° F. Butter an 8-inch x 8-inch baking dish.

Filling

Add the cherries, water, sugar, and cornstarch to a large saucepan. Stir the cherries well until the sugar and cornstarch are absorbed.

Heat the cherries on medium heat until they simmer. Reduce the heat. Simmer uncovered for 10 minutes. Stir the cherries as they simmer. Remove from the heat.

Crisp

Put the white sugar, brown sugar, flour, oats, cinnamon and salt in a large bowl. Whisk well. Add the melted butter into the dry mixture. Mix with a fork until the butter is absorbed. Sprinkle the topping over the fruit.

Bake for 25 to 30 minutes or until the topping is light brown and the fruit bubbles. Rotate the dish 180° halfway through cooking.

Remove from the oven and cool for 10 to 15 minutes.

Serve with ice cream or Sweetened Whipped Cream. (See the Sweetened Whipped Cream recipe in the Whipped Toppings Section).

Cherry Pistachio Crisp

Serves: 10 to 12+

Ingredients

Filling

8 cups pitted tart cherries

1/4 cup granulated sugar

1 tablespoon cornstarch

1 teaspoon vanilla extract

Crisp

1/2 cup all purpose flour

1/3 cup brown sugar

1/3 cup granulated sugar

1/2 teaspoon vanilla extract

6 tablespoons unsalted butter, chilled

1/2 cup shelled, unsalted pistachios, chopped

Directions

Heat the oven to 350 ° F. Butter a 9-inch x 13-inch baking dish.

Filling

Add the pitted cherries, sugar, cornstarch and vanilla extract. Mix well.

Pour the cherry mixture into the prepared baking dish.

<u>Crisp</u>

Sift the flour into a large bowl. Add the brown sugar, granulated sugar and vanilla extract.

Cut the butter into the flour mixture with a pastry blender until the mixture is pebbly.

Mix in the pistachios.

Spoon the topping evenly over the cherries.

Bake for 40 minutes to 50 minutes until the topping is light brown. Rotate the dish 180° halfway through cooking.

Take out of the oven and cool for 10 to 15 minutes.

Serve warm with ice cream or Sweetened Whipped Cream. (See the Sweetened Whipped Cream recipe in the Whipped Toppings Section).

Crunchy Apple Oatmeal Crisp

Servings: 6 to 8

Ingredients

3 to 4 Granny Smith apples (or other tart baking apples)
1 tablespoon lemon juice
1/2 cup flour
3/4 cup firmly packed brown sugar
3/4 cup quick cooking oatmeal
1 teaspoon cinnamon
1 teaspoon vanilla extract
1/2 cup unsalted butter

Directions

Preheat the oven to 350° F.

Butter an 8-inch x 8-inch baking dish.

Peel, core and thinly slice the apples. Put them in a large bowl. Sprinkle with the lemon juice and toss the apples.

Put the apples in the bottom of the baking dish and even them out with a spatula.

Sift the flour into a large bowl. Add the brown sugar, oatmeal, cinnamon and vanilla extract. Whisk until well-mixed.

Cut the butter into the flour-sugar mixture with a pastry cutter.

Sprinkle the flour mixture over the apples.

Bake in the preheated oven for 45 minutes or until the top has browned. Rotate the dish 180° halfway through cooking.

Take the crisp out of the oven and cool for 5 to 10 minutes.

Serve warm. You can serve the crisp plain, with Sweetened Whipped cream or ice cream. (See the Sweetened Whipped Cream recipe in the Whipped Toppings Section).

Peach Crisp

This is really more of an English crumble but it's delicious. It has a smoother topping made of flour, sugar, butter & spices.

Servings: 8 to 10

Ingredients

Filling
7 cups sliced peeled ripe peaches
1 teaspoon lemon juice
3 tablespoons all-purpose flour
1/4 cup packed brown sugar
1/2 teaspoon lemon zest
1/2 teaspoon ground cinnamon

Crisp
6 tablespoons unsalted butter, room temperature
1/4 cup light-brown sugar
1 cup all-purpose flour
1/4 teaspoon salt
1/2 teaspoon cinnamon
1/4 teaspoon nutmeg

Directions

Preheat the oven to 375° F.

<u>Filling</u>

Put the sliced peaches in a buttered 2-1/2-qt. baking dish. Sprinkle the lemon juice over the peaches and toss to mix.

Put the flour, brown sugar, lemon zest and cinnamon in a medium bowl. Whisk to combine.

Sprinkle the flour-sugar mixture over the peaches. Set aside.

<u>Crisp</u>

Put the butter and brown sugar into a mixing bowl. Using a mixer, beat the butter and brown sugar until light and fluffy.

Add the flour, salt, cinnamon and nutmeg to the butter-sugar mixture and mix until combined.

<u>Assemble the Crisp</u>

Spread the topping over the peaches.

Bake for 35 to 40 minutes or until the topping is light brown. Rotate the dish 180° halfway through cooking.

Remove from the oven and cool for 10 to 15 minutes.

Serve warm with ice cream or Brandy Whipped Cream. (See the Brandy Whipped Cream recipe in the Whipped Toppings Section).

Peach Raisin Crisp

Servings: 6 to 8

Ingredients

2-1/2 pounds fresh peaches, peeled, pitted
1 lemon, zested and juiced
1/2 teaspoon vanilla extract
1/2 cup golden raisins
1 cup sifted all-purpose flour
1/2 cup granulated white sugar
1/2 cup packed brown sugar
1/4 teaspoon salt
1/2 teaspoon cinnamon
1/2 cup soft unsalted butter

Directions

Preheat the oven to Preheat oven to 375° F.

Butter an 8-inch x 8-inch baking dish.

Slice the peeled and pitted peaches into chunks. Put the peaches into the prepared baking dish. Sprinkle with the fresh lemon juice and zest. Toss to mix.

Add the vanilla extract and raisins to the peaches. Stir until mixed.

Whisk together the flour, white sugar, brown sugar, salt and cinnamon into a large bowl.

Cut the butter into flour mixture with pastry blender until crumbly. Sprinkle the flour mixture evenly over the peaches in the baking dish.

Bake for 40 to 50 minutes or until the crust is light brown. Rotate the dish 180° halfway through cooking.

Remove from the oven and cool for 10 minutes.

Serve the peach crisp warm with ice cream or Sweetened Whipped Cream. (See the Sweetened Whipped Cream recipe in the Whipped Toppings Section).

Pear Crisp

Servings: 10 to 12+

Ingredients

<u>Filling</u>

3 pounds ripe pears, peeled and sliced
2 tablespoons lemon juice
1 tablespoon lemon zest
1/2 cup granulated sugar
2 tablespoons all-purpose flour
1/2 cup raisins
1 teaspoon crystallized ginger, minced

<u>Crisp</u>

1-1/2 cups rolled oats
1/2 cup packed brown sugar
1/3 cup all-purpose flour
1/2 teaspoon ground cinnamon
1/8 teaspoon ground ginger
Dash ground nutmeg
1/2 cup pecans, chopped
6 tablespoons unsalted butter, chilled

Preheat oven to 375°F. Butter a 9-inch x 13-inch baking dish.

<u>Filling</u>

Put the pears in a large bowl. Sprinkle with the lemon juice and lemon zest. Toss to coat.

In a separate bowl combine the granulated sugar, flour, raisins and crystallized ginger. Whisk to mix.

Add the sugar mixture to the pears. Mix well. Set aside.

Crisp

In a large bowl combine the rolled oats, brown sugar, flour, cinnamon, ginger, nutmeg and pecans. Mix well. Cut in the butter with a pastry cutter until the mixture is coarse.

Bake in the preheated oven for 40 to 45 minutes or until the topping is golden brown. Rotate the dish 180° halfway through cooking.

Remove from the oven and cool for 10 to 15 minutes.

Serve warm with ice cream or Brandy Whipped Cream. (See the Brandy Whipped Cream recipe in the Whipped Toppings Section).

Raspberry Crisp

Servings: 10 to 12+

Ingredients

Filling
4 cups raspberries, rinsed
1 teaspoon vanilla extract
3/4 cups sugar
2 tablespoons cornstarch

Crisp
1 cup all-purpose flour
1-1/3 cups quick oats
3/4 cup brown sugar
1/4 cup pecans, chopped
1/2 teaspoon baking soda
3/4 sticks cold unsalted butter, cut into thin pats

Directions

Preheat oven to 350° F. Butter a 9-inch x 9-inch baking dish.

Filling

Add 1 cup of raspberries to a medium bowl. Crush the raspberries. Add enough water to make 1 cup of combined raspberries and water.

Add the sugar and cornstarch to a large saucepan. Whisk to mix.

Stir in the 1 cup of raspberry-water mixture to the saucepan. Add the vanilla extract. Stir to mix.

Heat on medium and bring to a boil. Cook and stir for 2 minutes.

Stir in the remaining raspberries. Remove from the heat and cool.

Crisp

Add the flour, oats, brown sugar, pecans and baking soda to a large bowl.   Stir to mix.

Add the butter. Use a pastry cutter to cut the butter into the dry mixture until it's coarse and pebbly.

Assemble the Crisp

Pour the cooled raspberry mixture into the prepared baking dish. Sprinkle the topping mixture over the berries.

Bake for 30 to 35 minutes or until the topping is light brown. Rotate the dish 180° halfway through cooking.

Remove from the oven and cool for 10 to 15 minutes.

Serve warm with ice cream or Sweetened Whipped Cream. (See the Sweetened Whipped Cream recipe in the Whipped Toppings Section).

Raspberry Almond Crisp

Servings: 6 to 8

Ingredients

Filling

6 cups raspberries

1 teaspoon almond extract

1/2 cup sugar

Crisp

3/4 cup flour

2-1/4 cups oatmeal

1/2 cup almonds

3/4 cup unsalted butter

Directions

Preheat the oven to 400° F.

Butter an 8-inch x 8-inch square glass baking dish.

Filling

Mix the raspberries, almond extract and sugar in a large bowl. Turn the berry mixture into the baking dish.

<u>Crisp</u>

In a large mixing bowl whisk together the flour and oatmeal.

Cut the butter into the oatmeal-flour mixture with a pastry cutter. The mixture should be coarse.

Add the chopped almonds to the oatmeal mixture.   Stir well.

Sprinkle the oatmeal mixture over the top of the berries.

Bake for 35 to 45 minutes or until the topping is light brown. Rotate the dish 180° halfway through cooking.

Remove from the oven and cool for 10 minutes.

Serve warm with ice cream or Sweetened Whipped Cream. (See the Sweetened Whipped Cream recipe in the Whipped Toppings Section).

WHIPPED CREAM TOPPINGS

Almond Whipped Cream

Ingredients

1 cup heavy cream

2 tablespoons confectioners' sugar

1/2 teaspoon almond extract

Directions

Chill the mixing bowl and mixing beaters.

Pour the cream into the bowl.

Add the confectioners' sugar and almond extract.

Use an electric mixer to beat the cream until stiff peaks form.

Brandy Whipped Cream

Prepare this whipped cream right before serving.

Ingredients

1 cup heavy whipping cream, chilled

1 tablespoon brandy

4 tablespoons confectioners' sugar

Directions

Chill the beaters and the bowl. Whip the cream in the bowl on medium speed until it starts to thicken slightly. Add the brandy and confectioners' sugar and mix at medium-high speed until stiff peaks form. Don't overbeat the cream or it will separate. Serve right away for the best presentation and flavor.

If you need to refrigerate the whipped cream, put it in a bowl, cover with plastic wrap and refrigerate until you need it. Whisk the whipped cream before serving.

Lemon Whipped Cream

Ingredients

1 cup chilled heavy whipping cream

3 tablespoons powdered sugar

3 teaspoons fresh lemon juice

1 tablespoon lemon zest

Directions

Chill the beaters and the bowl. Beat the cream in the bowl on medium speed until it starts to thicken slightly. Slowly add the powdered sugar and continue to mix at medium-high speed. Add the lemon juice and beat until soft peaks form. Don't overbeat the cream or it will separate. Fold in the lemon zest.

If you need to refrigerate the whipped cream, put it in a bowl, cover with plastic wrap and refrigerate until you need it. Rewhisk the whipped cream before serving

Rum Whipped Cream

Prepare this whipped cream right before serving.

Ingredients
1 cup heavy whipping cream, chilled

3 tablespoons confectioners' sugar

1 tablespoon rum

Directions
Chill the beaters and the bowl. Whip the cream in the bowl on medium speed until it starts to thicken slightly. Add the confectioners' sugar and rum. Mix at medium-high speed until stiff peaks form. Don't overbeat the cream or it will separate. Serve right away for the best presentation and flavor.

If you need to refrigerate the whipped cream, put it in a bowl, cover with plastic wrap and refrigerate until you need it. Whisk the whipped cream before serving.

Sweetened Whipped Cream

Ingredients

1 cup heavy cream

2 tablespoons confectioners' sugar

1/2 teaspoon vanilla extract

Directions

Chill the mixing bowl and mixing beaters.

Pour the cream into the bowl.

Add the vanilla and confectioners' sugar.

Use an electric mixer to beat the cream until stiff peaks form.

Made in the USA
Lexington, KY
30 September 2013